High On A Hill!
A Kid's Guide To Innsbruck, Austria

Photography By John D. Weigand
Poetry By Penelope Dyan

Bellissima Publishing, LLC
Jamul, California
www.bellissimapublishing.com

copyright © 2011 by Penny D. Weigand

All rights reserved. No part of this book may be
reproduced or transmitted in any form or by any means,
electronic or mechanical, including photocopying,
recording, or by any other means, or by any information or
storage retrieval system, without permission from the publisher.

ISBN 978-1-935630-76-0

First Edition

"To hot dogs with freshly ground horseradish, and Wiener schnitzel with noodles."

Penelope Dyan

Introduction

Innsbruck, Austria is one of the most beautiful places in the entire world. High in the hills of Austria, you can get a feel of what it was like in the not too distant past, and in the old part of town, they have made great efforts to preserve what has made the town unique. Evidence shows habitation in the early Stone Age. Surviving pre-Roman place names show that the area has been continuously populated. Innsbruck is the capital city of the federal state of Tyrol in western Austria. It is located in the Inn Valley at the junction with the Sill River, and it provides access to the Brenner Pass, The word bruck comes from the German word Brücke which means "bridge." Innsbruck literally means "bridge over the Inn."

The Austrians and the people of Innsbruck have gone to a lot of trouble to make Innsbruck tourist and kid friendly. When you walk down the streets of the old part of the town, you almost feel like it was created by Walt Disney himself!

And even if you can't go to Innsbruck, you can still enjoy going there vicariously through the pages of this book with award winning author, attorney and former K-12 teacher, Penelope Dyan, and John D. Weigand, professional photographer and videographer,

Use the pages of this book to insert your own notes, photographs and tickets and things to make this book your very own; because it is only when you make a book your own that you can truly learn from its pages. Research, study and have fun; and if you go to Innsbruck see what you can recognize from this book! That will make your trip there even more interesting and fun, because you will be on a mission of discovery.

High On A Hill!
A Kid's Guide To Innsbruck, Austria

Photography By John D. Weigand
Poetry By Penelope Dyan

The first thing you see when you get into town,
is the beauty in the hills that is all around.
You'll see a church, and you'll see a steeple.
You'll think aloud, "What lucky townspeople!"

As for things to do you are not at a loss.
There is even a bridge that you can run across!
This is a place where discoveries abound.
With your two eyes they CAN be found.

You can take a walk with your
parents through this lovely park.
But do NOT go alone OR go when it gets dark.
There are yellow benches where you can sit,
if you happen to need to rest a bit.

You can take a horse and carriage
all the way to the old part of the town.
And you can rent a bicycle for one or two
and you can bicycle around!

If you want to get framed,
there's a picture frame made for you.
(Go sit inside.)
People do it all the time!
And it's a lot of fun to do!

The Hungerburgbahn* is something to see.
You can take it to Hungerburg quite easily.

＊ The Hungerburgbahn is not "exactly" part of the public transit. You have to pay a surcharge to use it. It is a stand-alone system shuttling people from the city centre of Innsbruck to the Alpine suburb of Hungerburg and is a"Hybrid" Funicular system.

Through a stone arch is the
old part of the city.
Everything is unique.
And it's really quite pretty.

You can buy toys there
and hats and dolls and things.
You can buy necklaces, scarves,
bracelets and rings!

There are Lederhosen* made for boys.

* Lederhosen is German for leather breeches or pants. Lederhosen are trousers that are made short or knee-length.

There are things for the ENTIRE family,
even instruments that make a GRAND noise!

The buildings are so colorful on each and every street.

You will see Column Annasaule.*

* The column "Annasaule" is located in the middle of the Maria Theresienstrasse in the city centre of Innsbruck. The monument was built to celebrate the liberation from the Bavarians on July 26, 1703.

And you can get something really good to eat!*

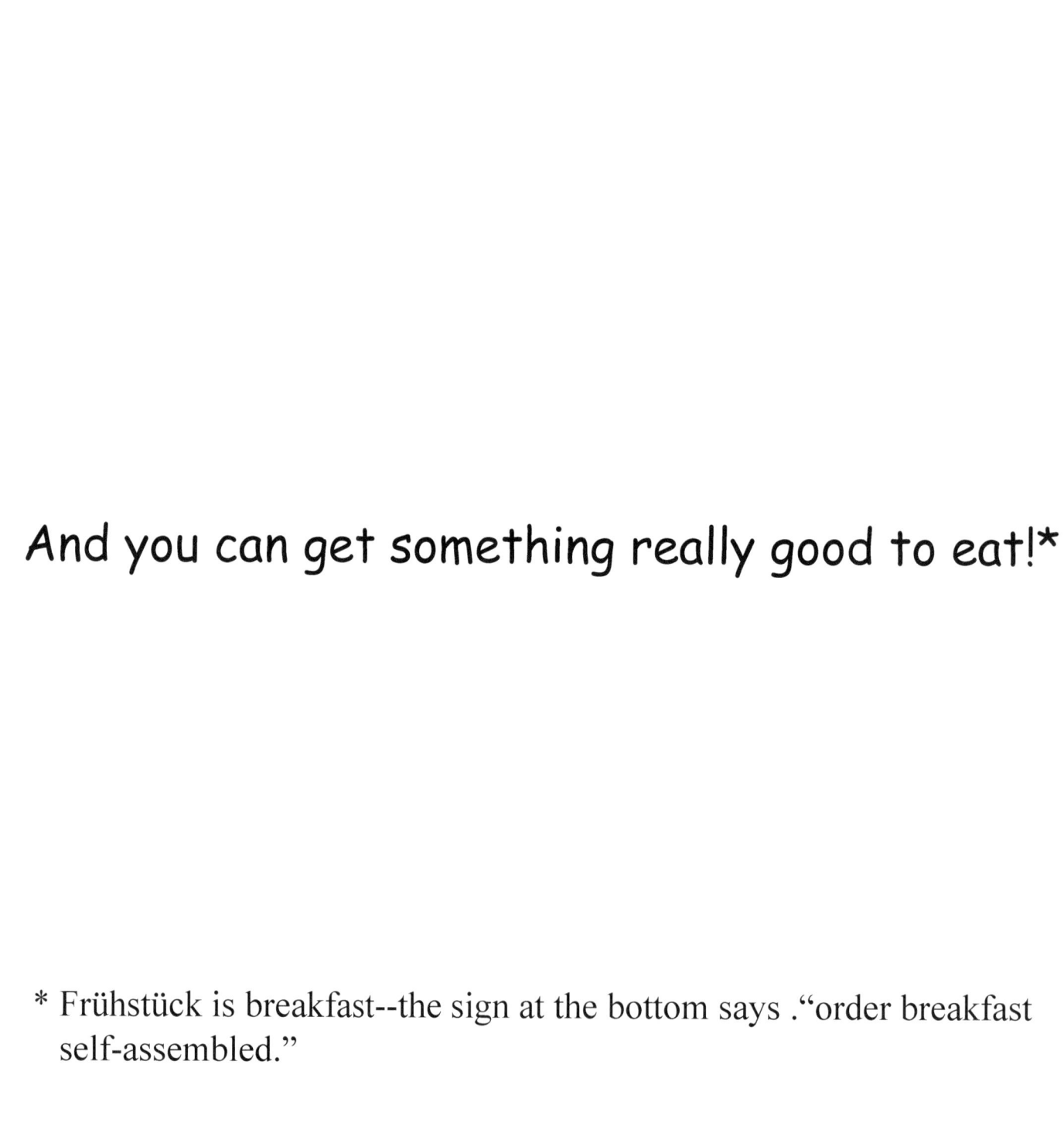

* Frühstück is breakfast--the sign at the bottom says ."order breakfast self-assembled."

And finally (much later)*
when the clock strikes three
you'll think there is no more to see.

* The clock now says 10:10 AM.

Then you'll see a roof embellished in gold.*
You'll be told that it is very old.
And as it glimmers in the sun,
you'll think to yourself, "This day has been fun!"
You bought a toy and something sweet,
and brand new slippers for your tired feet.
Soon you'll go back to your hotel and hop in bed.
And upon a soft pillow you will rest your head.

* Innsbruck Golden Roof--The Golden Roof in the old town of Innsbruck is the most important symbol of the city. Archdruke Friedrich IV built the roof for Emperor Maximilian I in the 15th century in honor of Maximlian's second marriage.

"The real voyage of discovery consists not in seeking new landscapes, but in having new eyes."

Marcel Proust
10 July 1871 – 18 November 1922

www.ingramcontent.com/pod-product-compliance
Ingram Content Group UK Ltd.
Pitfield, Milton Keynes, MK11 3LW, UK
UKHW060137240426
12048UKWH00002B/71